Al Jaffee

GAGS

Written, illustrated, and regurgitated by Al Jaffee

A SIGNET BOOK
NEW AMERICAN LIBRARY
TIMES MIRROR

SIGNET TRADEMARK REG. U.S. PAT. OFF. AND FOREIGN COUNTRIES
REGISTERED TRADEMARK—MARCA REGISTRADA
HECHO EN CHICAGO, U.S.A.

SIGNET, SIGNET CLASSICS, MENTOR, PLUME and MERIDIAN BOOKS are published by The New American Library, Inc., 1301 Avenue of the Americas, New York, New York 10019

First Printing, November, 1974

3 4 5 6 7 8 9

PRINTED IN THE UNITED STATES OF AMERICA

DEDICATION

To that certain someone, without whose tireless inspiration and support this book would not have been possible . . . and you know who THAT is.

Two Forewords for the Price of None

Al Jaffee's Fold-In, on the inside back cover of every issue of MAD, is a certainty on a par with death, taxes and Labor Day, and just as unavoidable and as celebrated.

Recently, I saw a gal I would have liked to know carrying two bags of groceries and a newly purchased MAD. Standing stork-like and balancing one of the bags on a raised knee, she paused to comply with the "A" MEETS "B" instructions on the MAD Fold-In. No stranger to Jaffee's tantalizing tuck-and-go feature, apparently, she made an adroit one-handed crossover crease of the page. Through the ingenious "Close sesame!", the deliberately deceptive scene reproduced from Jaffee's vibrant acrylics was transformed into a meaningful symbol. The related question atop the page was answered tersely and trenchantly at the bottom of the page. Every calculated camouflage, every mental and visual agitation, every fake-out in phraseology, every bit of sleight of brush Jaffee infuses into each Fold-In, is designed to produce the surprise and exhilaration of an emerging notion! The revitalized lovely with the groceries grinned and shook her head: How does Jaffee do it!

That isn't all Jaffee does in MAD and for MAD.

His renowned "Snappy Answers To Stupid Questions" are the snide and searing antibodies that purge one's system of the anemic queries that should have gone unasked.

And when Jaf offers us quasi-solutions and facetious devices to counteract canine-induced pavement pollution, or to foil second-story men whittling away at our ground floor or on our roof, or to dissuade and isolate inconsiderate smokers, his master plans entail the seeming workability of Patent Pending.

Al Jaffee's constantly requested Hate Books that appear regularly in MAD alleviate us of the little loathes that are big pains. *Don't You Hate . . .* dentists with hairy arms! *Don't You Hate . . .* hot drinks served in paper cups! *Don't You Hate . . .* gas station attendants who insist on "rounding out" the amount of your purchase so you end up paying for gas that overflowed onto the ground!

My estimable fellow mortal, Associate Editor Nick Meglin, and I have been privileged to roam the foothills of the Olympus that is MAD. From that height of creativity emanate celestial graphics and exalted continuity. Al Jaffee continues that tradition in this book. Speaking of our Olympus, Al Jaffee may very well be its Zeus.

But don't take my word for it. Just ask Nick Meglin...

Jerry De Fuccio

Jerry De Fuccio
Associate Editor
MAD Magazine

Talk about tough acts to follow, Jaffee—Olympus—Zeus? Jerry, MAD's token gentleman, *would* say something like that—something kind, something flattering, something phoney! He'd do no less for Hitler. Zeus indeed! Well, dear reader, I'm sorry to be the balloon-buster around here, but I know Al Jaffee too, or better, Al Jaffee TWO, since there seems to be more than one. The Al Jaffee I know is a creep! Who else would ask you to write a foreword "as a favor" when we all know he's just too cheap to pay for someone *good* to write it! If you go with Jaffee to a coffee shop and have coffee, and maybe a donut, he'll say in a loud voice so everyone in the joint can hear—"It's on me, Al Jaffee!" Then, when you're in a steak house with him and the check comes, he directs the waiter over to you and says, "It's your turn—I got it last time!"

And steal ideas! Having a script conference with Jaffee is like playing your brain back on a tape recorder! Everything you ever said finds its way into one of his books or articles. One day I told him, "You know what I hate? Guys who steal other guys' ideas!" Two days later at a script conference Jaffee presents a new Hate Book idea, the first example being, "Don't you hate guys who hate other guys using their ideas?" Don't you think he sold us the article? What's even worse, *I* voted for it!

And appreciation? None! Zero! I first spotted Jaffee

as an asphalt stomper, stomping barefoot over the hot asphalt on a First Avenue construction job. I bought him a suit, a pair of shoes, a tie, I teach him how to draw, I showed him how to use his suit and tie and shoes and drawings to get a job and make a better living for himself. Now that he's a big shot in the field and getting invited to parties, I'm not a big enough shot to get an invitation for, is it right that when someone asks him, "How's Nick?" he answers, "Nick who?" I mean really, is that right? Is that a nice thing to do?

So let Jerry use the *big words* and say the *right thing* and be the *nice guy.* Jerry's a gentleman (although I could say a few things about that guy too if I wanted to!). But I'm just the kind of slob that tells it to you like it is, which is why I only write forewords. For books by creeps like Al Jaffee. For free, no less. Zeus indeed!

Nick Meglin

Nick Meglin
The other Associate Editor
MAD Magazine

CHAPTER 1

The big blow-up

Pop!

POP!

POP!

POP!

CHAPTER 2

A witless collection of wordless whimsicalities

POLICE

CHAPTER 3

Smokey the unbearable

Wow! Wait'll you see what I can do with this cigar.
Watch this.
2
3

4

5

POP!
Well, what are you going to do with the cigar?
I know what I'd **LIKE TO** DO with the cigar.
6

CHAPTER 4

The old shell game

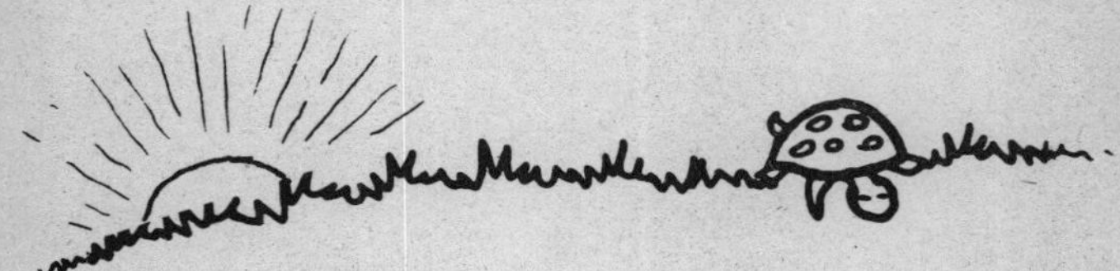

2

3

4

5

Speed
crazy
kid.

CHAPTER 5

Another painful batch of bungled buffooneries

OASIS
MIRAGE
DANCING
GIRLS
MIRAGE

Easter already? How time flies.

There's where defense spending **economies** get you.

I was voted "most likely to succeed" in school and I'd have made it if it weren't for that lousy bank alarm.

Your job, Smedley, is to see to it that customers feel Finchley's cares about their problems. Now let's see how you handle this old bat.
ADJUSTMENTS
SALE

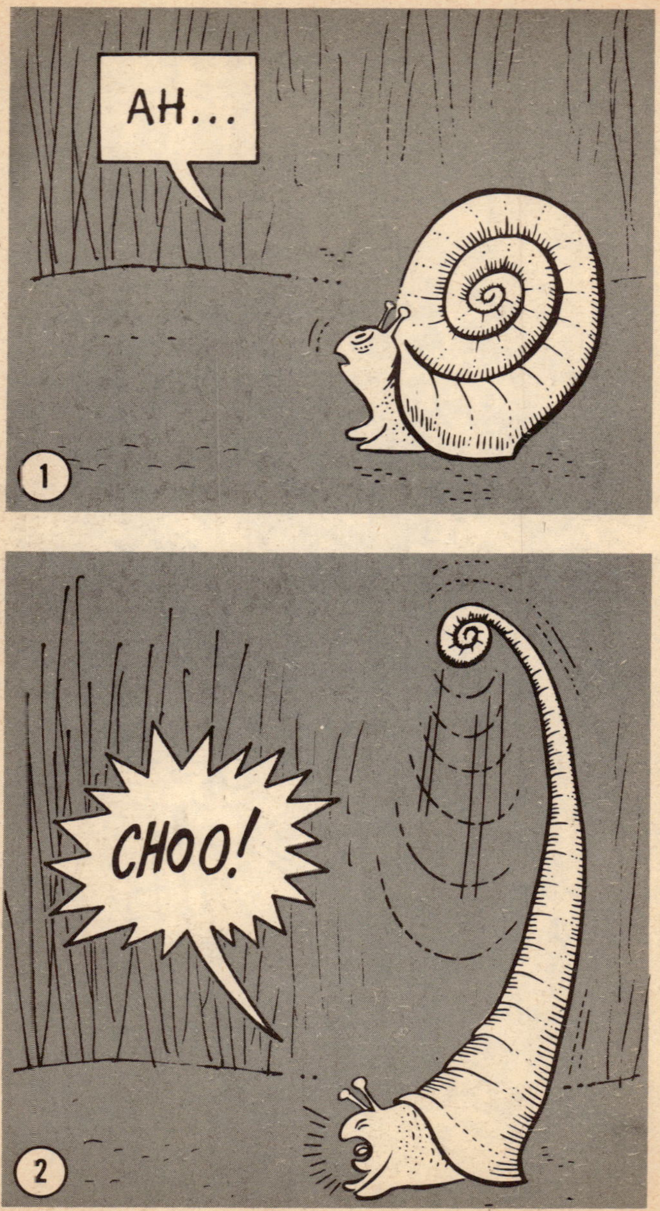

AH...

1

CHOO!

2

WHEW!!
SQUEEZE LEFT

CHAPTER 6

The last word

1

. . . and furthermore, I work and slave day and night around here, but is there ever a word of **appreciation?**
NO!
2

Is there ever an act of kindness, a show of grati-
tude, a small token of consideration?
NO! NO! NO!

FLORIST
SAY IT WITH FLOWERS
4

5

7

CHAPTER 7

Another disturbing cluster of tiresome trivialities

ED & LIL'S NURSERY
I don't care what they say about people who live in glass houses . . .

A leader should get out into the field with his men. Good for morale, you know.

The way the economy has been going, that fortune I stashed away will be worthless when I get out.

YOWIE
I think daddy's found your submarine, Freddy.

1

There's certainly
no sign of life
on this planet.

2

Sorry. I was just showing my son how to use his new trampoline.

CHAPTER 8

The big come down

1

2

This magnificent statue
is dedicated to our
glorious achievements
and general excellence
in every field of endeavor.

3

4

5

CHAPTER 9

Humor in a light vein

2

3

CHAPTER 10

Another distressing accumulation of jumbled jocularities

I know they have a highly organized society but this is ridiculous.
NO U TURN
FULL STOP
ONE WAY
ONE WAY

CRACK!

Who the hell
has been using
my electric
toothbrush?

NUTS

NICK MEGLIN! What in blazes are you doing in this neck of the woods?

How did I know it was his first job? He said, "Mand over the honey and you hon't wet gurt!"

What's the excuse this time, Frisbee . . . and make it a good one!

CHAPTER 11

A noteworthy event

2

One more chance.
Get it right, or
get out.

4

OKAY, OUT!
5

6

CHAPTER 12

Another irritating clutch of burdensome banalities

GUARD
GUARD

TELEPHONE
LUCKY
NUGGET
CASINO

Lucky, devil.
I believe you've
struck oil.
DEPT.

MIAMI

DAVID FRAZIER NEWS CO.

Well, how does it feel to finally have a child in college?
BEAN
OIL

Remember. We've got to keep each other's spirits up or we'll both go nuts.

EASTERN AUTO RENTALS
CURRENT LOCATION OF CARS
It's on a ferry.

FRANK
'N'
DRINK
60¢
Yeah, I got the raise and I'm blowing it all on lunch.

CHAPTER 13

A reel life drama

2

3

6

CHAPTER 14

Another galling compilation of contrived comicalities

I suggest you go home and change your shirt, Bedlow.
Yutzville GUN CLUB

QUICK
SAND
1

SLOW
~~QUICK~~
SAND
2

WATCH FOR GRAND OPENING!
GLAZIER
I want great big windows because I like a lot of light.
1

SHOP MART
BIG SALE
%30 OFF
COME IN AND SAVE
TODAY ONLY
$1
2 for 50¢
AZIER
2

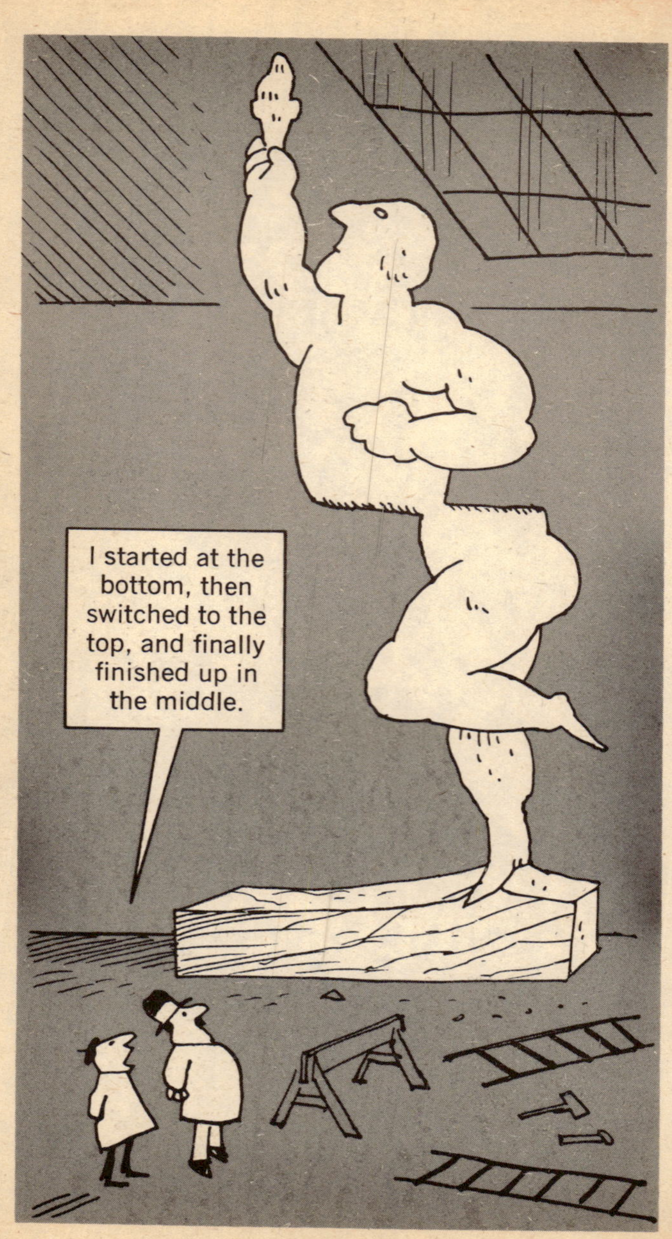
I started at the bottom, then switched to the top, and finally finished up in the middle.

WINDUP
ANIMALS
$ 1.00

MATERNITY
Don't get excited, Mr. Birdwell. It's only laundry.

CHAPTER 15

A tight spot

2

3

4

5

6

CHAPTER 16

Another pitiable roundup of ridiculous risibilities

YOWEEE!
A hole
in one!

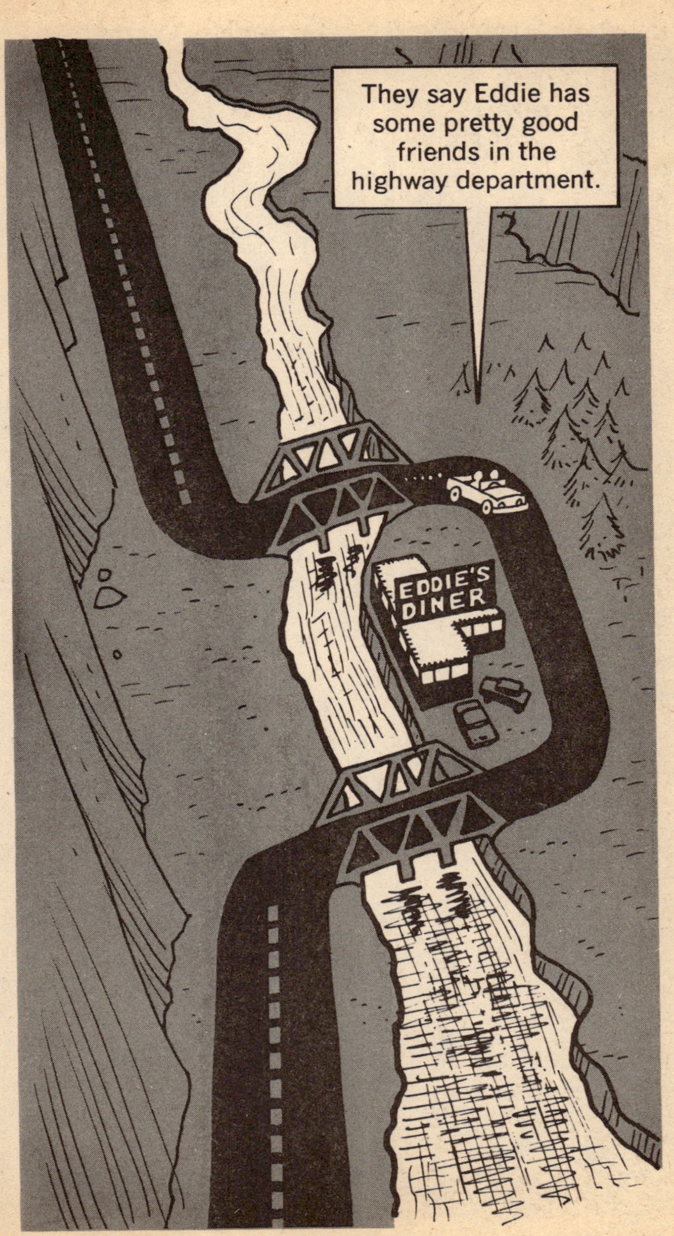
They say Eddie has some pretty good friends in the highway department.
EDDIE'S DINER

You'll just have to buy a grater . . . I can't afford to be late for rehearsal again.

SAL'S
SHOE
REPAIRS

PRISON
HOBBY
SHOP
60735

I don't understand it . . . they're supposed to be fiercely hostile.

CHAPTER 17

One dark and dreary knight

2

3

4

6

CHAPTER 18

Another disagreeable conglomeration of dimwitted drolleries

Give me one good reason why carrying passengers in trailers needs to be illegal.

Why in blazes didn't you say you were start-ing at the top.

AMBULANCE
Stop complaining . . . you're lucky it was us.

There's not a thing wrong with you that a little fun and relaxation won't cure.

If he thinks the soup tastes like dishwater, let's see what he thinks **THIS** tastes like.

TROPICAL FISH

SERGEANT MAJORS

. . . and let's
not have any
low blows.

He wasn't a bit of trouble.

CHAPTER 19

An out of sight saga

ELECT
J. PUTNAM
2

3

4

5

BRENNER'S
AUTO
DRIVING
SCHOOL
6

CHAPTER 20

Another lamentable quantity of meaningless merriments

Tsk, tsk, tsk.
The cost of living
has gone up again.

. . . but before we begin our dictation for today, a word from our sponsor. . . . Do you suffer from "OVERSLEEP"? Do you get to your office late every day? Do you worry about losing your job? . . .

I hope whomever it belongs to **can't see** long enough for us to get the hell out of here.

And now . . .
the hard way.

I can't believe anything could happen today to make me feel any worse than I already do.

A lot of the old values are lost when the young people return from the white man's school, Neeneenanoo.

That convertible
you sold me just
converted itself
into a piece
of junk.

Now here's a really good shot of the baby.

Naw, fishing's terrible here.
Try the other side of the lake.
BAIT

CHAPTER 21

A sucker story

1

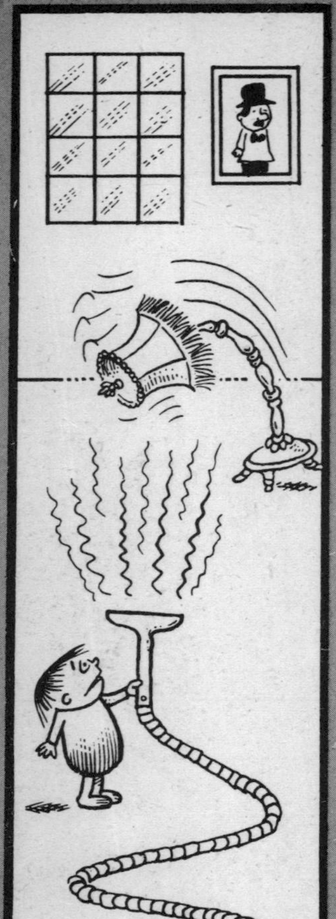

VACUVAK

2

VACUVAK

3

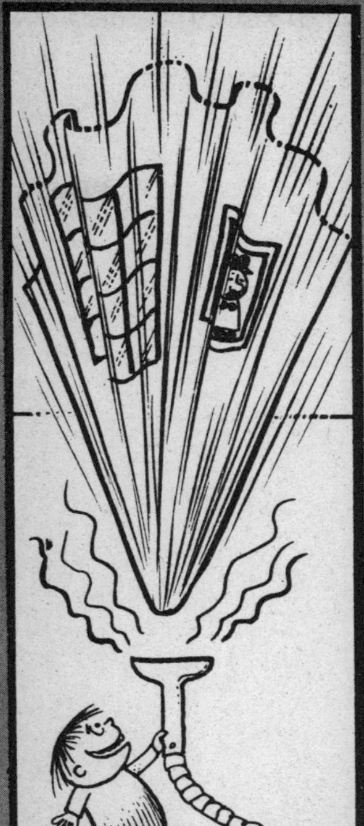

4

5

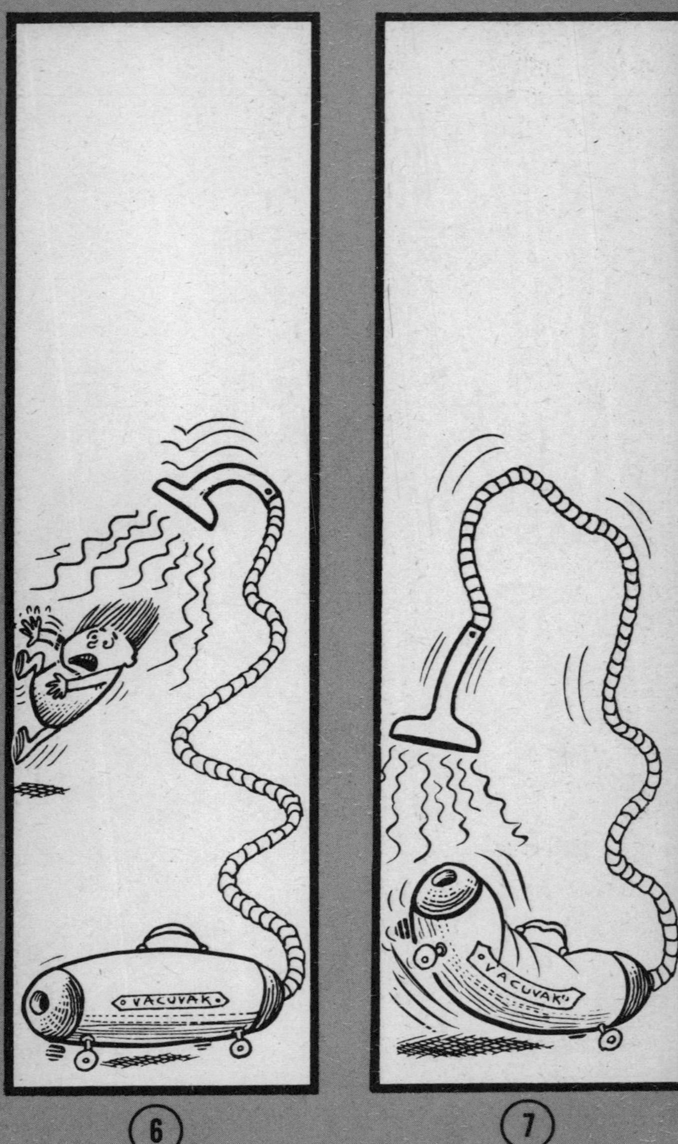
VACUVAK
6
VACUVAK
7

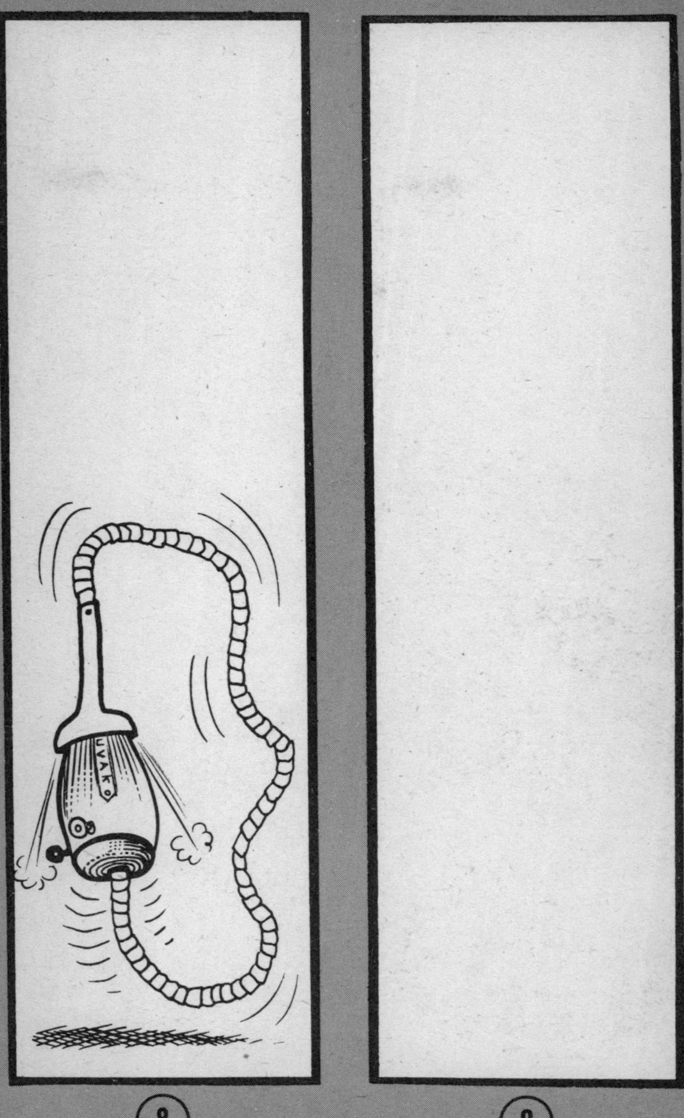

8

9

CHAPTER 22

A heady experience

1

2

3

4

CHAPTER 23

Another aggravating aggregation of irksome irrelevancies

She's with the circus.

I've been expelled from school.

Hello, Fister Towing Service? My car's stuck right smack in the middle of . . . uh, never mind.
TELEPHONE
STOP
R.R. CROSS

Dad, have you by any chance seen my pet porcupine?

MEDICAL
SUPPLIES

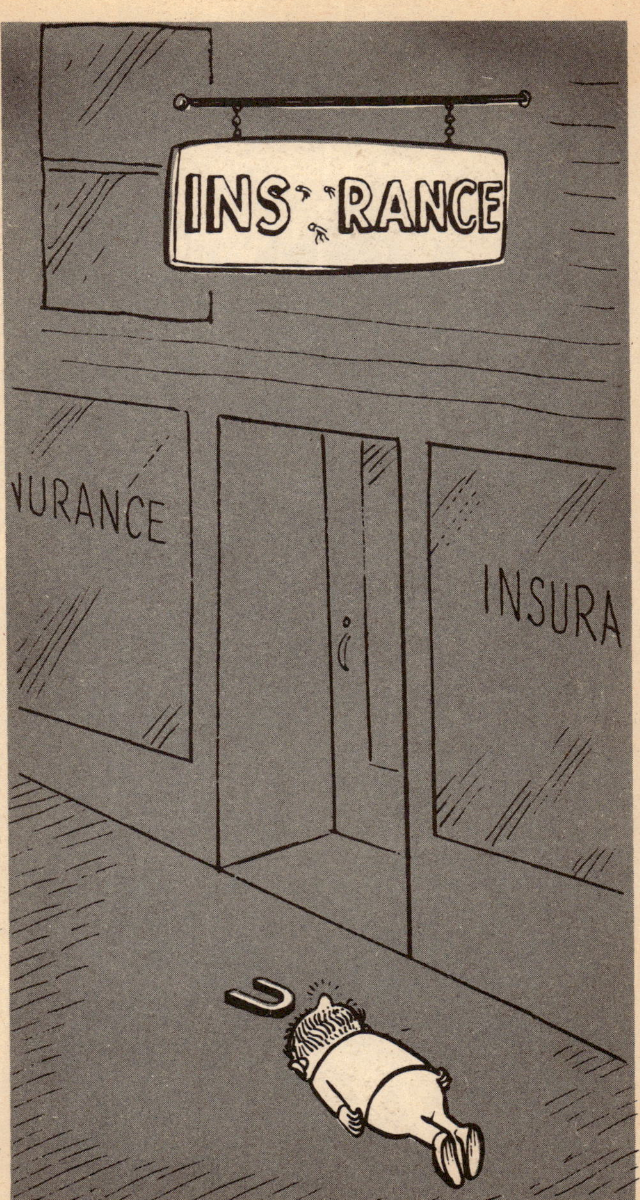
INS RANCE
URANCE
INSURA

Now aren't you glad you switched from the violin to the bass fiddle?

I really shook him up with, "What are you, a man or a mouse?"!
? ? ?

I can't stand a show-off.

CHAPTER 24

Bugged bothered and bewildered

HA! MISSED
2

MISSED AGAIN
BUG-DED
3

CLOSE, BUT NO CIGAR
4

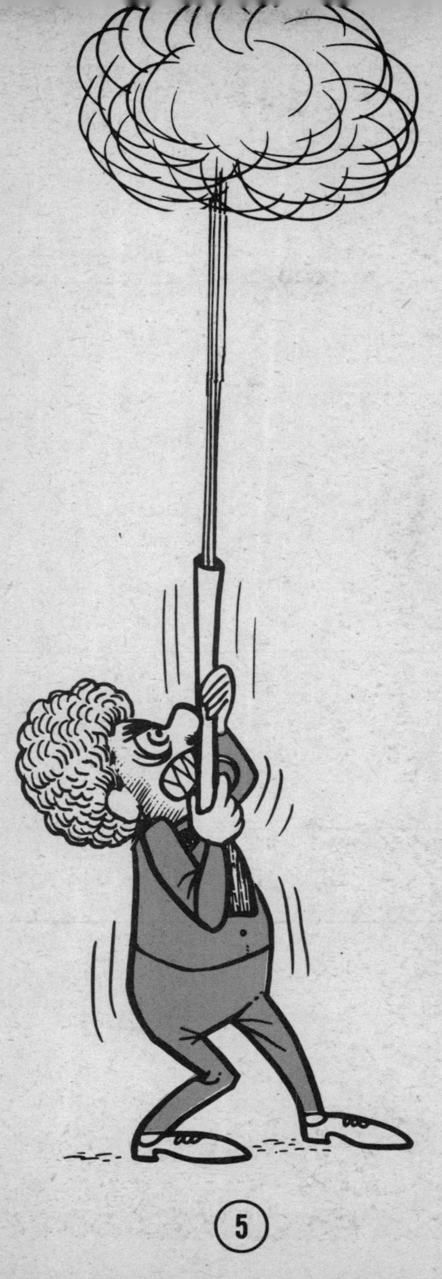
5

ARGHHH... YA GOT ME
6

7

8

CHAPTER 25

A final assemblage of pointless prankeries

PUBLIC LIBRARY

ONE WAY

DEER
CROSSING

What did you expect him to look like? He IS a baboon.

. . . of course, if you select special option six. . . .

1

. . . you'd be fully insured against the following hazards . . .

2

He finally cracked after eight straight hours of daytime TV.

MARRIAGE COUNSELOR
Tell me in your own words just how the trouble starts.
Well . . .
I'll tell it!

THE END OF THE
WORLD, WHICH
WAS SCHEDULED
FOR YESTER-
DAY, HAS BEEN
POSTPONED
INDEFINITELY
DUE TO LAST
MINUTE TECH-
NICAL DIFFI-
CULTIES. WATCH
THIS SPACE FOR
FURTHER DE-
VELOPMENTS.